Pebble® Plus

Investigate the Seasons

Let's Look at Spring

Revised Edition

by Sarah L. Schuette

CAPSTONE PRESS
a capstone imprint

Pebble Plus is published by Capstone Press,
1710 Roe Crest Drive, North Mankato, Minnesota 56003
capstonepub.com

Library of Congress Cataloging-in-Publication Data
is available on the Library of Congress website.

ISBN 978-1-5435-0858-1 (library binding)
ISBN 978-1-5435-0874-1 (paperback)
ISBN 978-1-5435-0878-9 (ebook pdf)

Editorial Credits
Sarah Bennett, designer; Tracy Cummins, media researcher,
Laura Manthe, production specialist

Photo Credits
Capstone Studio: Karon Dubke, 15; Shutterstock: Catalin Petolea, 21,
Dmitry Strizhakov, 17, fotohunter, 9, Liubou Yasiukovich, Cover Design
Element, Mariola Anna S, 7, Pakhnyushchy, 1, PCHT, Cover, RaJi, 13,
shahreen, 11, StripedNadin, 3, Sunny Forest, 19, WH CHOW, 5

Note to Parents and Teachers

The Investigate the Seasons set supports national science standards
related to weather and life science. This book describes and
illustrates the season of spring. The images support early readers in
understanding the text. The repetition of words and phrases helps early
readers learn new words. This book also introduces early readers to
subject-specific vocabulary words, which are defined in the Glossary
section. Early readers may need assistance to read some words and to
use the Table of Contents, Glossary, Read More, Internet Sites, Critical
Thinking Questions, and Index sections of the book.

Table of Contents

It's Spring!

How do you know

it's spring?

Spring is full of life.

Bright sunlight shines.

The next day rain falls.

Spring days are warmer
and wetter than winter days.

Sun and rain help

plants grow.

Everything is green again.

Animals in Spring

What happens

to animals in spring?

Birds feed their young

in nests.

Sheep graze

in green pastures.

Newborn lambs walk

on wobbly legs.

Plants in Spring

What happens to plants

in spring?

Tulips bloom.

Grass grows.

Blossoms cover cherry trees.

Bees buzz in and out

of the flowers.

Planting begins on farms.

Rows of crops

sprout in fields.

What's Next?

The weather gets warmer.

Spring is over.

What season comes next?

Glossary

blossom—a flower on a fruit tree or other plant

crop—a plant grown in large amounts; corn, wheat, soybeans, and oats are some crops planted in spring

graze—to eat grass that is growing in a field

pasture—a field of grass where animals graze

season—one of the four parts of the year; winter, spring, summer, and fall are seasons

sprout—to start to grow

wobbly—unsteady

Read More

Owen, Ruth. *How Do You Know It's Spring?* Signs of the Seasons. New York: Bearport Publishing, 2017.

Pettiford, Rebecca. *Spring.* Seasons of the Year. Minneapolis: Bellwether Media, 2018.

Rotner, Shelley. *Hello Spring!* New York: Holiday House, 2017.

Internet Sites

Use FactHound to find Internet sites related to this book.

Visit *www.facthound.com*

Just type **9781543508581** and go.

 **Super-cool stuff!** Check out projects, games and lots more at **www.capstonekids.com**

Critical Thinking Questions

1. What helps plants grow?

2. Describe two signs that it is spring.

3. How is spring different from winter?

Index